Sheila Campbell

SIDE HUSTLE

&

PASSIVE INCOME

Sheila Campbell

Sheila Campbell

Copyright @ 2024 by Sheila Campbell

Table of contents

X. Conclusion

A. Recap of Key Points

B. Encouragement for Taking Action

Introduction

First of all, Those who are keen to change their financial story might find guidance in the quest of side gigs and passive income in a world where financial independence and flexibility are highly valued. Welcome to "Side Hustles and Passive Income," a comprehensive manual designed to help you achieve financial independence.

With the intention of demystifying the worlds of side gigs and passive income, this booklet functions as a comprehensive road map. It provides you with the knowledge, tactics, and doable actions you need to successfully traverse the terrain of supplemental revenue streams. This guide is your partner in the quest for financial resilience, regardless of your goals—building a diverse portfolio, augmenting your existing income, or escaping the 9–5 grind.

Side Hustle

A side hustle is an additional source of income that someone pursues in addition to their regular job or career. It is usually a part-time endeavor that gives people the chance to follow their passions, learn new skills, and—most importantly—make extra money in addition to their primary work.

Passive Income

Earnings produced with little to no active participation or effort on the part of the recipient are referred to as passive income. Passive income streams can arise from investments, company initiatives, or assets that continue to create cash with no continuous effort, in contrast to typical employment, where active work is required to make money. People who generate money passively while not working can achieve a certain level of financial liberty.

It is vital to diversify sources of income for multiple reasons:

1. Risk Mitigation: You lessen reliance on a single revenue stream by distributing money among several sources. Your finances are better protected by this diversification against unforeseen events, recessions, and difficulties unique to your business.

2. Stability and Consistency: Having a variety of revenue sources contributes to a more steady financial base. In the event of a setback for one source, others might still contribute, guaranteeing a more steady total revenue.

3. A Chance for Development:

The presence of several revenue sources creates room for expansion. You can take on a variety of projects, invest in a range of assets, and investigate new business opportunities, which may lead to future growth and higher profits.

4. Adaptability to Change: Industries and economic environments change. With multiple sources of income, diversification enables you to adjust to changing circumstances.

5. Economic Adaptability:

By reducing reliance on a single source of income, diversification increases financial flexibility and gives individuals the freedom to follow their personal or professional interests. A lifestyle that is more balanced and satisfying may result from this freedom.

6. Economic Stability Over Time:

Creating a varied portfolio of sources of income is one way to ensure long-term financial stability. It supports your financial objectives, such as retirement, investments, or big-ticket savings, by building a strong financial safety net.

Essentially, diversifying sources of income is a proactive approach that reduces risks, strengthens financial stability, and lays the groundwork for long-term, sustainable prosperity.

CHAPTER 1

Understanding side Hustle and passive income

Types of side hustle:

Freelancing:

One exciting side business is freelancing, which is selling your abilities and services to clients on a project-by-project basis. Here's how to pursue freelancing as a side gig using this guide:

1. Identify Your Skills: Ascertain your main competencies and areas of strength. This might be anything from graphic design and writing to marketing, programming, or any other particular knowledge you have.

2. Build a Portfolio: Compile your finest work into a portfolio. Provide references, case studies, and other pertinent experience to show prospective customers how knowledgeable you are.

3. Select a Platform: Connect with clients seeking freelance services by signing up for freelance platforms like Upwork, Fiverr, or Freelancer. Make changes to your profile to emphasize your qualifications and experience.

4. Describe Your Offerings: Clearly describe the services that you provide. Include any special features that make you stand out from other freelancers in your industry, along with the deliverables and scope of work.

5. Decide on Your Rates: Based on elements including your experience, the project's complexity, and industry norms, determine your pricing structure. Be open and honest about your prices to gain your clients' trust.

6. Craft Strong Suggestions: When submitting a proposal for a freelancing job, make sure it addresses the needs of the customer specifically. Emphasize how your abilities meet the needs of the project.

7. Skillful Interaction: Keep lines of contact with clients open and transparent. Answer messages right away, ask questions as necessary, and give regular updates on the status of the project.

8. Time Management:

Manage your time well in order to fulfill deadlines. Make sure that everyone knows when you are available, and establish reasonable deadlines for doing the job.

9. Create Connections:

Delivering excellent work and acting professionally in all of your interactions can help you build strong relationships with your clients. Client satisfaction increases your chances of being hired again or having referrals for you.

10. Ongoing Education:

Keep up with changes in the industry and periodically refresh your skills. This keeps you competitive in the market for independent contractors.

Utilizing your expertise, working on a variety of tasks, and having the freedom to choose when and where you work are all made possible by freelancing. Freelancing can grow into a lucrative and long-lasting side gig with commitment and initiative.

B.   CONSULTING

Consulting is a flexible side business where people use their experience to give clients insightful counsel and direction. This can be done in a variety of sectors. The following is an outline of how consulting can be done as a side gig:

1. Define Your Niche: Specify your area of knowledge and specialty. In every sector, be it finance, marketing, IT, or any other, having a specific area of expertise adds credibility.

2. Establish Your Own Brand:

Create a professional online presence by using social media profiles or a website. Present your abilities, background, and accomplished endeavors to draw in possible customers.

3. Networking: Take an active part in offline and online networking. Join professional associations, go to industry events, and make connections with possible partners or clients.

4. Offering Services: Clearly state what kind of consulting services you provide. This could be creating strategies, fixing problems, providing training, or working in any other particular field where clients need help.

5. Gig Marketplaces:

Investigate freelance marketplaces where people and companies can find consultants. Finding consultancy opportunities can be facilitated by using platforms such as Upwork or Freelancer.

6. Client Acquisition: Create tactics for acquiring clients that work. This might be contacting companies directly, setting up introductory meetings, or producing informative content to highlight your areas of expertise.

7. Determining Fees:

Based on your experience, industry norms, and the value you provide to clients, establish your consulting prices. Be open and honest about your pricing policy.

8. Time Management: Strike a balance between your main obligations and consultancy. To properly manage your time, clearly define the scope of the activity and set reasonable deadlines.

9. Ongoing Education:

Keep abreast with market developments and work to improve your abilities constantly. A competent consultant is in a better position to offer clients insightful advice.

10. Relationships with Clients:

Develop a relationship with your clients by giving them outstanding service, staying in touch, and communicating clearly. Client referrals and recurring business are likely to come from happy customers.

GIG ECONOMY JOBS

Taking on gig economy work provides a flexible and diverse way to make money. Here's how to take advantage of side gig opportunities in the gig economy:

1. Explore Platforms: Look into and sign up for gig economy platforms that fit your hobbies and skill set. Task-based platforms like TaskRabbit, food delivery services like DoorDash or Uber Eats, and ride-sharing services like Uber or Lyft are a few examples.

2. Create a Profile: On the selected platform, create an engaging profile. Provide pertinent information about your background, abilities, and any qualifications that are necessary for the particular position.

3. Understand needs: Become acquainted with each gig's needs. This could involve background checks, car specs, or other requirements needed to do the tasks.

4. Flexible Scheduling: Make the most of the flexibility provided by gig economy jobs to arrange your schedule in a way that aligns with your main responsibilities. You can work when it's most convenient for you thanks to your flexibility.

5. Service to Customers:

Give exceptional customer service first priority. Your chances of getting hired again in the future might be greatly impacted by positive evaluations and ratings.

6. Financial Planning: Recognize the payment schedule and make appropriate financial plans. While some gig economy jobs pay instantly, others have a weekly or monthly payment schedule.

7. Precautionary Steps:

Take precautions, particularly if your job requires you to travel or engage with people physically. Respect the platform's rules and take the appropriate safety measures to protect your health.

8. Spread Across Gigs:

Examine the different gig options available in the gig economy. For example, if you drive for a ride-sharing company, think about expanding your horizons by taking on additional jobs like food delivery.

9. Make Use of Referral Programs:

Benefit from the referral schemes that certain gig marketplaces provide. By referring new drivers or users, you may be eligible for extra rewards or incentives.

10. Remain Updated:

Keep abreast of any modifications to the gig economy environment, such as the introduction of new platforms, laws, or fashions. With this information, you may maximize your revenue and gig selections.

B. Assessing Interests and Skills for Potential Side Projects:

When thinking about side business ideas, it's critical to carefully evaluate your hobbies and skill set. This is a step-by-step method to help you match your skills to possible side projects:

1. Introspection:

Consider your abilities, both personal and professional, for a while. Determine your strongest suit and think about things you actually enjoy doing.

2. List of Skills:

Make a thorough inventory of all the abilities you possess, including transferrable, soft, and technical skills. This can include specialized technical know-how as well as strong organizational, communication, and problem-solving ability.

3. Interests and Passions:

Enumerate your interests, passions, and hobbies. Consider the extracurricular pursuits that make you happy and fulfilled in addition to your primary job.

4. Determine Transferable Skills:

Determine which of your abilities are in demand or marketable. Think about the potential uses of these abilities in a side business.

5. Look at Possible Side Jobs:

Look into several side gigs and see which ones fit your hobbies and skill set. For instance, selling digital artwork or freelancing could be realistic possibilities if you have graphic design talents.

6. Evaluate Demand: Take into account the market for goods and services that are a fit for your expertise. If there is a market need for what you offer, your side project has a better chance of becoming successful.

7. Explore New Skills: Have an open mind to learning new abilities if they are required for a certain side project. Your skill set can be expanded through self-directed study, workshops, and online courses.

8. Assess Time Commitment:

Determine how much time you can actually devote to a side business. Certain endeavors can need more time up front, while others provide greater flexibility.

9. Take into Account Market Trends:

Keep up with market developments and new business prospects. This might assist you in determining any possible skill-related shortages in the market.

10. Trial and Error: Begin with a smaller project or try out several side gig concepts. This enables you to evaluate what best aligns with your interests, abilities, and market need.

11. Ask for Feedback: Consult mentors, colleagues, or possible clients for their opinions. Their observations can offer insightful viewpoints on how marketable your abilities and side project ideas are.

CHAPTER 2

Setting up a side Hustle

The process of creating and setting up the fundamental components required to start and run a profitable side business is referred to as "Setting Up a Side Hustle" in this chapter. To ensure the side project grows and is sustainable, this entails taking legal issues into account, drafting an extensive business strategy, and developing a strong online and offline presence. In order to establish the foundation for a successful and organized side gig, readers should follow the chapter's instructions.

A. Legal consideration:

Establishing a side business requires understanding and taking care of legal issues. This entails navigating a variety of legal requirements and making sure that pertinent regulations are followed. Important elements consist of:

1. Organizational Structure:

Select a suitable business structure, such as a corporation, LLC, partnership, or sole proprietorship. The legal ramifications for responsibility, taxes, and regulatory compliance vary depending on the structure.

2. Registration and Licensing: Verify and complete any licensing or registration procedures specific to your side business. This could entail registering your company name, getting the required licenses, or following rules unique to your sector.

3. Tax Obligations: Recognize your responsibilities with regard to taxes as a business owner. This include obtaining a business tax ID, maintaining correct financial records, and paying all applicable local, state, and federal taxes.

4. Agreements & Contracts:

Create detailed and unambiguous contracts for your goods and services. Contracts give transactions with customers, suppliers, or partners a legal basis, help set expectations, and safeguard your interests.

5. Intellectual Property Protection:

Find and safeguard any patents, trademarks, or copyrights that are connected to your side business. This prevents unlawful use of your original artwork or products.

6. Observance of Labor Laws:

Be mindful of and abide by employment rules if your side project entails recruiting staff or using contractors. This entails being aware of labor laws, working conditions, and minimum pay standards.

7. Privacy and Data Protection:

Put policies in place to safeguard consumer information and follow privacy regulations. Create a privacy policy that describes the procedures for gathering, utilizing, and protecting consumer data.

8. Insurance Coverage: Take into account getting insurance that is pertinent to your side business. Depending on your sector, this could include professional indemnity insurance, liability insurance, or other types of coverage.

9. Local and Zoning Regulations:

Pay attention to any local ordinances and zoning requirements that can affect your side project, particularly if it requires operating out of a certain site. Make sure all zoning regulations are followed, and get any required permissions.

10. Dispute settlement: Ensure that your contracts include a dispute settlement procedure. Provisions for mediation, arbitration, or other dispute resolution procedures with clients may be included in this.

Creating a business plan

An essential first step in starting a side gig is creating a thorough business strategy. A business plan outlines your objectives, tactics, and the general organization of your enterprise, acting as a roadmap. Important elements in writing a business strategy consist of:

1. Executive Synopsis:

Give a succinct description of your side project, emphasizing its goals, mission, and purpose. Your business plan's introduction is provided in this part.

2. Description of the Business:

Describe the nature of your side business, the goods or services it offers, and the issue it seeks to resolve. Clearly state your target market and unique value proposition.

3. Analysis of the Market:

Become well-versed about your target market, industry, and rivals. Determine consumer demands, market trends, and possible obstacles to help guide your business plan.

4. Constitutional Framework:

Describe the structure that your side project will follow. Indicate the main roles and duties for all team members and partners in the project.

5. Goods or Services:

Describe in full the services your side business offers. Give an explanation of the attributes, advantages, and cost of your goods and services.

6. Sales and Marketing Plan:

Create a strong plan for sales and marketing. Specify how you will market your side project, connect with your target market, and turn leads into paying clients.

7. Monetary Forecasts:

Make thorough financial estimates that include a break-even analysis, cash flow forecasts, and income statements. Describe your possible sources of finance and any financial requirements you may have.

8. Analysis of SWOT

Perform a SWOT analysis (Strengths, Weaknesses,

Opportunities, Threats) in order to determine the potential internal and external influences on your side business. Make use of this analysis to improve your tactics.

9. Operational Plan: Describe how your side project is run on a daily basis. Provide details on the suppliers, the production procedures, the technology needed, and any necessary digital or physical infrastructure.

10. Risk Management: Recognize possible hazards and create plans to lessen them. This can include shifts in the market, modifications to regulations, or unforeseen difficulties.

11. Schedule and Checkpoints:

Create a schedule for your side business that includes important dates. This makes sure you stay on pace to reach your goals and helps you monitor your progress.

12. Exit Strategy: Even if it's a side gig, think about possible ways to get out of it. Whether you intend to wind down the company, sell it, or transfer ownership to a successor, having a well-defined exit strategy offers a long-term outlook.

In addition to providing guidance for the beginning of your side project, a business plan is an invaluable resource for continuing decision-making and strategy modifications. As your side project develops, revisit and revise your business strategy on a regular basis.

Establishing a Robust Online Presence:

In the current digital era, having a good online presence is essential to the success of your side project. This entails using a variety of internet media, engaging with your target audience, and presenting your brand strategically. Important actions to create an internet presence include:

1. Website Creation: Create a polished, user-friendly website that accurately conveys your brand, provides key information, and is search engine optimized.

2. Using Social Media: Choose appropriate social media networks according to your target market and participate regularly on sites like Facebook, Instagram, LinkedIn, and Twitter. Make your material specific to each platform.

3. Strategies for Content Marketing:

Provide informative and useful information in the form of blog entries, articles, videos, and infographics. By sharing your knowledge, you might become recognized as a thought leader in the field.

4. Search Engine Optimization (SEO):

By adding pertinent keywords, producing high-quality material, and making sure technological elements improve search engine rankings, you may optimize your website and its content for search engines.

5. Email Marketing Implementation: Create an email list and run email marketing campaigns to stay in touch with your audience on a regular basis by sending out promotions, updates, and helpful material.

6. Encouraging Reviews and Testimonials: To increase credibility, encourage happy customers to post reviews and testimonials on review sites relevant to your business or on sites like Yelp or Google.

7. Maintaining Visual Brand Consistency: For unified recognition, develop a consistent visual brand identity that includes a logo, color palette, and imagery that are in line with your brand principles.

8. Considerations for Online Advertising: To boost visibility and reach a wider audience, assess online advertising options on sites like Google Ads, Facebook Ads, or other pertinent channels.

9. Encouraging Community Engagement: To create a feeling of community around your brand, actively participate in your online community by leaving comments, sending direct messages, and creating interactive content.

10. E-commerce Integration if Applicable: If your website allows it, use e-commerce features to help clients make direct transactions and have a simpler purchasing experience.

11. Mobile Optimization Focus:

Make sure your website is mobile-friendly to improve the experience of users who are reaching your brand via tablets or smartphones.

12. Continuous Analytics and Observation:

Use analytics software to track metrics such as website traffic and social media interaction in order to keep an eye on your online performance.

CHAPTER 3

Maximizing passive income

"Maximizing Passive Income" in this chapter refers to investigating and putting into practice methods for maximizing the creation of revenue streams requiring little continuous work or direct participation. The emphasis is on finding and seizing opportunities to increase the effectiveness and profitability of passive income sources, which include investments, digital goods, and other ventures that continue to generate returns while requiring less active involvement on the side of the investor.

Explaining Passive Income:

The idea of passive income in finance refers to profits that are made with little continuous work or direct participation. Passive income streams, in contrast to traditional types of income obtained via active labor, enable people to collect money through a variety of sources that yield returns over time. Investments, rental income, dividends, royalties, and internet enterprises are a few examples of these sources.

The attraction of passive income is its capacity to offer people financial security and independence, enabling them to accumulate money while lowering their reliance on active labor. Understanding and utilizing passive income requires investigating many options, making wise investments, and developing self-sufficient assets.

how to diversify and effectively manage revenue streams to build long-term, sustainable financial prosperity.

Investments:

Investments involve allocating capital with the expectation of generating returns over time. Key elements include:

1. Asset Classes: Investments span diverse classes such as stocks, bonds, real estate, and mutual funds. Diversification helps manage risk.

2. Risk and Return: The relationship between risk and potential return varies. Higher-risk investments may yield greater returns, but they come with increased uncertainty.

3. Stock Market: Investing in stocks means owning a share of a company. Stock prices fluctuate based on market dynamics, company performance, and economic conditions.

4. Bonds: Bonds are debt securities where investors lend money to entities, receiving periodic interest payments and the return of principal at maturity.

5. Real Estate: Real estate investments involve purchasing property for rental income or capital appreciation.

6. Mutual Funds: Professionally managed stocks, bonds, and other assets are invested in by mutual fund pools, which combine the money of several individuals.

7. Exchange-exchanged Funds (ETFs): ETFs are investment funds that are exchanged on stock exchanges; they provide flexibility in intraday trading together with a diversified approach akin to mutual funds.

8. Spreading Out:

Reducing risk can be achieved by distributing investments among several assets. Potential gains and losses are balanced in a well-diversified portfolio.

9. A Long-Term View:

Having a long-term outlook is generally necessary for successful investing. Although markets might be unpredictable, compound gain can be achieved with patience.

10. Research and Due Diligence: Careful investigation and diligence are necessary for making well-informed decisions. Making strategic decisions is aided by having a solid understanding of investing principles.

Dividends and Stocks

1. Stocks: - Stocks are a symbol of ownership in a business. Owners of stocks, sometimes referred to as shares or equities, become shareholders and are entitled to a share of the assets and profits of the business.

- A number of variables, including market conditions, economic trends, and corporate performance, affect stock values.

Preferred investors frequently receive fixed dividends but may not have voting rights, whereas common stockholders may be able to vote on business decisions.

2. Dividends: - A firm distributes dividends to its shareholders, which are a fraction of its profits.

- Dividends are usually paid in cash, but they can also be given out as extra stock or other assets.

- Regular dividend payers are viewed as stable and financially sound businesses, which draws in income-seeking investors.

One important statistic for income investors is dividend yield, which is computed as the annual dividend per share divided by the stock price.

When weighing prospective capital growth against consistent income, investors frequently take a combination of growth and dividend companies into account. A thorough understanding of dividends and stock dynamics is necessary to make wise investing choices.

Real Estate

Purchasing and maintaining properties for a variety of financial objectives is the nature of real estate investing. Important real estate investing factors are as follows:

1. Types of Real Estate Investments:
- Residential: Single-family homes, apartments, or vacation properties.

- Commercial: Retail establishments, office buildings, and industrial assets.

- Real Estate Investment Trusts (REITs): Investment vehicles that finance, own, or manage real estate across a range of industries that generates income.

2. Rental money: Renting out houses to renters is a popular way to generate rental money.

- Rental yield is a measure of return that is computed by dividing annual rental income by the value of the property.

3. Capital Appreciation: - As properties increase in value over time, investors may benefit from a sale.

Property values are influenced by market movements, location, and demand.

4. Financing: - Mortgages are a common way for investors to leverage their real estate investment when financing real estate purchases.

- The total returns are affected by loan terms, interest rates, and financing options.

5. Property Management: - Good administration is essential. This covers upkeep, managing tenant relations, and attending to any legal or regulatory obligations.

- Companies that manage properties can help with daily operations.

6. Diversification: - Adding real estate to an investment portfolio diversifies it and lowers total risk.

- The risk-return profiles of various properties or places differ.

7. Crowd funding for Real Estate - Through platforms, investors can pool money for real estate projects, giving them access to a variety of investment options with lower capital needs.

8. Risks: - Investing in real estate entails risks such market swings, recessions, and difficulties unique to a given property.

It is crucial to conduct due diligence on the property's condition, market trends, and location.

9. Tax Considerations: - Tax benefits for real estate investors include capital gains tax treatment, mortgage interest deductions, and property depreciation.

10. Market Analysis: - Before making an investment, thoroughly analyze the market. Take into account variables such as local economic conditions, demographics, and job growth.

Investing in real estate can result in income, capital growth, and portfolio diversification. To invest successfully in real estate, one must have a deep understanding of its subtleties and perform extensive study.

Producing and Market Digital Goods:

Digital product creation and sales are profitable side businesses that use technology to provide useful tools or information. Important elements of this side business consist of:

1. Digital Products: - These comprise audio files, software, templates, e-books, and online courses, among other things. These are intangible goods that are simply sent to clients via electronic means.

2. Content Creation: - Provide valuable, high-quality content that solves a particular problem or offers a solution.

- Content can come in a variety of forms, including textual materials, interactive software, audio files, and video tutorials.

3. Platform Selection: - Select digital product selling venues, such as e-commerce sites, your own website, or niche platforms for particular product categories.

 - Popular sites are Amazon for e-books, Udemy for courses, and Etsy for digital art.

4. Payment Processing: - To make transactions easier, set up safe payment processing techniques. Using payment gateways like PayPal, Stripe, or other e-commerce solutions may be necessary for this.

5. Promotion and Marketing: - Create a marketing plan to advertise your digital goods. To reach your target audience, make use of partnerships, email marketing, content marketing, and social media.

- To draw clients, provide sales, discounts, or one-time deals.

6. Customer Support: - Offer first-rate customer service to quickly resolve any questions, concerns, or requests.

Think about developing tutorials or a FAQ area to help users of your digital items.

7. Protection of Intellectual Property: - Clearly state the license agreements, copyright policies, and conditions of usage pertaining to your digital items.

- Guard your intellectual property to avoid dissemination or usage without permission.

8. Alteration and Feedback: - Solicit client input to enhance your offerings. Utilize endorsements and evaluations to establish trustworthiness.

- Maintain the relevance of your digital products and cater to customer needs by updating or improving them frequently.

9. Diversification: - To reach a wider audience, diversify the digital products you offer.

To provide options for various client categories, think about bundling products or implementing tiered pricing.

After the first effort is completed, the creation and sale of digital items allows for scalability and the possibility of passive revenue. You can create a long-lasting and lucrative side business in the digital marketplace by consistently improving your goods and marketing strategies.

CHAPTER 4

Balancing Act- Managing full-time work and side hustles

The goal of this chapter, "Balancing Act," is to help readers navigate the opportunities and problems that come with pursuing a side project and a full-time job at the same time. The chapter looks at time management techniques, work-life balance, and productivity optimization techniques to help you have a successful and long-lasting dual career. The appropriate balance, overcoming obstacles, and accomplishing goals in both main career and side hustle ventures will be revealed to readers.

Time-Management Tips:

Having a side business and a full-time work at the same time requires efficient time management techniques. Take note of these pointers to make the most of your schedule:

1. Prioritize Tasks: - Determine which are most important for your side project and full-time employment. Concentrate on the most productive tasks to increase output.

2. Set Clear Goals: - Make sure both roles have definite, attainable goals. This gives you guidance and keeps your attention on the important things.

3. Make a Schedule: - Make a reasonable timetable that allots specific time for your personal life, side project, and full-time work. Try your best to adhere to this schedule.

4. Time Blocking: - Use time blocking to set aside particular amounts of time for various tasks. This guarantees that each position receives focused attention while reducing outside distractions.

5. Learn to Delegate: - Assign work to others when you can. Delegating well can reduce workloads and boost productivity, whether at work or in your side project.

6. Use Productivity Tools: - Organize yourself, manage deadlines, and streamline activities by utilizing productivity tools and apps. To-do list apps, project management tools, and calendar apps are useful.

7. Establish Reasonable Expectations: - Regarding what you can do in a specific amount of time, be realistic. A healthy pace is maintained and burnout is avoided by setting reasonable expectations.

8. Set Boundaries: - Make sure that clients, coworkers, and collaborators are aware of your boundaries and availability. Establishing expectations lowers tension and avoids misunderstandings.

9. Batch comparable jobs: - Assign comparable jobs to one another and work on them in blocks of time. This reduces context switching and increases productivity.

10. Regular Breaks: - Arrange brief pauses to rejuvenate. Even a quick break from work might help focus more clearly and keep burnout at bay.

11. Assess and Modify: - Consistently review your time management techniques. If some strategies aren't working, be willing to make changes and improvements.

12. Learn to Say No: - Set priorities for your work based on your objectives. Refuse politely any more commitments that can make your schedule too busy.

13. Prime Time: - Set aside time for intimate pursuits and self-nurturing. A strong work-life balance is necessary to juggle side projects and employment.

14. Contact is Crucial: - Maintain regular contact with your employer and partners in your side project. Open communication promotes comprehension and assistance.

15. Celebrate Achievements: -

Note and commemorate significant anniversaries and accomplishments in your side project as well as your full-time employment. Seeing progress increases one's motivation.

By putting these time management strategies into practice, you may increase productivity, preserve a positive work-life balance, and handle the responsibilities of both your side project and full-time employment.

Preventing Burnout:

When running a side business and a full-time work at the same time, it's important to avoid burnout. Put these tactics into practice to protect your health:

1. Set Realistic Expectations: - Make doable plans and refrain from taking on more than you can do. Setting reasonable goals helps people avoid burnout and reduce stress.

2. Prioritize Self-Care: - Include self-care as an essential component of your daily schedule. Make rest, fitness, and sleep your top priorities to revitalize your body and mind.

3. Plan Downtime: - Set aside time for rest and breaks. Make time for rest and rejuvenation during your schedule.

4. Learn to Delegate: - Assign work to others when you can. Realize that you don't have to manage everything on your own, in your side project as well as at work.

5. Create Boundaries: - Establish distinct lines separating your personal life, side business, and work life. Refrain from working long hours and spend time on non-work-related hobbies.

6. Take Short Breaks: - Spread out your daily pauses throughout the day. Short breaks help minimize mental weariness and help you clear your head.

7. Celebrate Achievements: - No matter how tiny, take pride in and acknowledge your accomplishments. Acknowledging accomplishments raises spirits and staves against burnout.

8. Regular Assessments: - Evaluate your obligations and workload on a regular basis. In the event that burnout manifests, take prompt action to address the underlying reasons.

9. Learn to Say No: - Exercise caution while accepting new commitments. Refuse opportunities or projects that can take up too much of your time in a courteous manner.

10. Interaction with Employers: - Keep lines of communication open with your boss. Talk about issues with workload and look into ways to control expectations.

CHAPTER 5

Analyzing What Works: Unraveling the Success of Side Hustles

Success in the world of side gigs is mostly dependent on knowing what works. Through analyzing and explaining the essential components that make successful side gigs successful, people can obtain insightful knowledge that will help them on their own entrepreneurial path.

1. Identification of Niche Opportunities: - Finding niche opportunities in the industry is sometimes the first step in starting a successful side business.

- Because they are acutely aware of gaps or unfulfilled needs, entrepreneurs are able to customize their side projects to meet particular needs.

2. Strategic Time Management:

- A strategic approach to time management is shown through the analysis of profitable side ventures.

Entrepreneurs exhibit a thorough planning approach by allocating their time wisely and striking a balance between their previous obligations and side projects.

3. Adaptability and Flexibility: - A common feature of successful side gigs is the capacity to change course and pivot.

- Entrepreneurs remain aware of market trends and modify their products and services to suit changing needs and conditions.

4. Effective Marketing and Branding:

- Strong marketing and branding initiatives are frequently revealed when examining successful side projects in more detail.

- Entrepreneurs are skilled communicators of value propositions, using a variety of media to connect with and engage their target market.

5. Customer-Centric Approach: - The success of many side projects is largely dependent on the happiness and involvement of the customer.

Understanding their clients, getting feedback, and refining their goods and services in response to client preferences are top priorities for entrepreneurs.

6. Leveraging Digital Platforms: - Using digital platforms becomes a unifying factor.

- Effective side projects increase their influence and reach by utilizing the marketing, sales, and community-building capabilities of online platforms.

7. Diversification of Income Streams: - Successful side projects frequently look at a variety of revenue sources.

- To reduce risk and build a stronger financial base,

entrepreneurs diversify their products or sources of income.

8. Investment in Skill Development:

- Successful side hustlers make ongoing investments in their skill sets. This dedication helps them be flexible and innovative in their endeavors, whether they are learning new talents or honing their current ones.

9. Community Building and Networking: - Creating a welcoming environment and strategically utilizing networking opportunities are common themes.

- Online and off, entrepreneurs cultivate relationships to build a network that not only supports their side business but also provides access to chances for growth and collaboration.

10. Persistence and Resilience:

- Successful side gigs require both persistence and resilience.

- Entrepreneurs are tenacious in overcoming obstacles, taking lessons from failures and utilizing them as stepping stones to success.

Through the examination of profitable side ventures, people can extract practical guidelines and understandings. Gaining success with a side hustle requires a variety of skills, including grasping market dynamics, honing time management techniques, and embracing adaptability. These findings clear the way for wise and calculated decision-making.

CHAPTER 6

Beyond Obstacles

In this chapter, "Overcoming Challenges," we examine the several roadblocks and difficulties people face when pursuing side gigs. This chapter dives into real-life examples, methods, and helpful advice from people who have navigated and triumphed over hurdles in the pursuit of their side hustles. These problems range from time limits to financial demands and unanticipated losses. By learning about problem-solving techniques, resilience, and the perseverance needed to overcome setbacks, readers will be better equipped to face their own difficulties head-on.

Typical Roadblocks for Side Projects:

Side projects frequently present their own share of difficulties. It's critical to identify and comprehend these typical roadblocks in order to successfully navigate the entrepreneurial journey. The following are some difficulties that people commonly face:

1. Time restrictions: - Time restrictions might arise from juggling a side business with a full-time work and personal obligations.

- It can be difficult to find time for the side project in between other responsibilities.

2. Financial Pressures: - Many side hustlers face difficulties with funding and money.

- A lack of resources may make it more difficult to invest in the side business or handle unforeseen expenses.

3. Uncertain Market Conditions: - Variations and uncertainties in the market might have an impact on a side business's ability to succeed.

- Outside variables that are out of the entrepreneur's control could affect competitiveness or demand.

4. Work-Life Balance: - Keeping a good work-life balance is a constant struggle.

Striking a balance between your personal life, career, and side project takes deliberate work.

5. Customer Acquisition: - One of the most frequent challenges is bringing in and keeping consumers.

- It can be difficult to develop a customer base and create a steady flow of revenue, particularly in areas with lots of competition.

6. Skill Gaps: - Mastering the abilities required for the side gig can be challenging.

- There could be a learning curve for entrepreneurs in fields like technology, finance, or marketing.

7. Competition: - Many side hustlers find it difficult to compete in crowded markets.

- Strategic positioning is necessary to set your side project out from the competition.

8. Isolation and Support: - It's common to struggle with feelings of isolation or a lack of support.

- The support system of a typical company may be missed by side hustlers, therefore it's important to look for it elsewhere.

9. Scaling Challenges: - Growing a side business comes with its own set of difficulties.

It's possible for entrepreneurs to run into issues with employment, growth, and operational scalability.

10. Regulatory Compliance: - Complying with regulations and maintaining compliance can be challenging.

It's crucial to make sure the side project complies with applicable laws and industry rules.

11. Marketing Effectively: - For many side giggers, developing and implementing an efficient marketing plan might be difficult.

- It may require some trial and error to determine the most effective messaging, channels, and targeting strategies.

Entrepreneurs can proactively address and overcome hurdles on their side hustle journeys by acknowledging these frequent obstacles. Through strategic problem-solving, resilience, and adaptation, people can overcome these obstacles and succeed more in their entrepreneurial endeavors.

Methods for Overcoming Obstacles in Side Projects:

Failures are a part of every entrepreneurial endeavor. The following are techniques to handle and get past obstacles in your side business:

1. Reflect and Learn: - Give the setback some thought and consider the factors that led up to it.

Determine what may be improved upon and what lessons might be learnt to guide future decisions.

2. Maintain a Positive Mindset: -

Develop an optimistic outlook to deal with setbacks with fortitude.

- See obstacles as chances for development and education.

3. Adaptability and Flexibility: -

Adopt a flexible mindset and embrace adaptability.

- Modify your plans or strategy in light of the lessons you've learnt from failures.

4. Seek Feedback: - Consult colleagues, mentors, or clients for their opinions.

- Outside viewpoints can offer insightful analysis and possible fixes.

5. Break Down Challenges: - Divide the obstacle into more doable, smaller tasks.

- Take care of each element one at a time to avoid being overwhelmed.

6. Prioritize Solutions: - Give attention to solutions rather than focusing on the issue at hand.

- Rather than dwelling on the setback per se, concentrate on doable strategies to get over it.

7. Reevaluate Goals: - In light of setbacks, reevaluate your long- and short-term objectives.

- Modify objectives to take into account newly acquired knowledge and the actual situation.

8. Network and Collaborate: - Make use of your network to get assistance and work together.

- Talk about failures with mentors or peers who can provide support or advice.

9. Resource Optimization: - Make the most of the time, money, and talents that you have at your disposal.

Determine which regions could benefit from resource reallocation or more effective use.

10. Build Resilience: - Develop resilience as a crucial quality for overcoming obstacles.

- Create coping strategies to overcome obstacles and emerge from them stronger than before.

11. Celebrate Small Wins: - Along the journey, recognize and commemorate little victories.

Acknowledging accomplishments despite obstacles keeps motivation high.

12. Reassess and Adjust Strategies:

- Review your entire strategy and make any required modifications.

- Be willing to make adjustments to your product offers, marketing strategy, or business model.

13. Take Strategic Risks:

- Evaluate the possible advantages of taking strategic chances to get beyond obstacles.

- Rigorous risk-taking can result in creative answers or expansion prospects.

14. Diversify Income Streams:

- To lessen the impact of setbacks, think about diversifying your sources of income.

- Several sources of income can offer stability in trying times.

15. Self-Care and Mental Health:

- Give self-care top priority if you want to be emotionally and mentally well.

- Implement procedures that support stress management and a positive work-life balance.

By putting these techniques into practice, people can overcome obstacles and use them as chances to grow and progress in their side hustle path.

Chapter 7

Scaling Your Side Hustle into a Business

In "Scaling Your Side Hustle into a Business," we explore the life-changing process of turning a side project into a fully fledged company. This chapter offers insights into the crucial processes and factors to be taken into account while growing, by examining growth plans, operational scalability, and strategic decision-making. Through helpful guidance, inspiring tales of success, and doable suggestions, readers will be able to navigate the thrilling and demanding process of turning their side project into a profitable and long-lasting business endeavor.

Finding Areas for Development

Discovering and seizing possibilities for growth is essential when turning your side project into a company.

Here's a calculated method to find potential growth areas:

1. Market Analysis:

- Carry out in-depth market research to pinpoint new trends and unfulfilled demands.

Examine consumer inclinations and actions to make sure your products and services meet market needs.

2. Customer input:

- Use client input to identify areas that need development and improvement.

  - Interact with your audience to learn about possible improvements to your product or service.

3. Diversification of Offerings:

- Consider broadening the range of goods and services you provide.

  - Find supplementary goods or services that fit your brand and serve your current clientele.

4. Target New Audiences: - Determine and focus on fresh clientele.

- Modify your marketing tactics to reach untapped markets and broaden your market penetration.

5. Strategic Partnerships:

- Look for joint ventures or influencer relationships.

- Work together to open up new markets, build credibility, or jointly develop cutting-edge products.

6. Digital Expansion:

- Increase your internet visibility by utilizing digital channels.

Investigate digital marketing, social media, and e-commerce platforms to expand your audience.

7. Geographic Expansion: - Take into account branching out into other regions.

Evaluate markets that have comparable demographics or have

unrealized potential for your goods or services.

8. **Optimize Operational Efficiency:** - To improve operational efficiency, streamline internal procedures.

Determine opportunities for cost-cutting, resource-saving, and automation.

9. **Marketing Invested**:

- Step up marketing initiatives to build brand recognition.

- To increase visibility, spend money on SEO, content marketing, and targeted advertising.

10. Technology Integration:

- Use technology to enhance customer experiences and business procedures.

Investigate cutting-edge technologies including data analytics, CRM software, and e-commerce platforms.

11. Franchising or Licensing:

- If your business plan lends itself to it, look into franchising or licensing prospects.

   - Grow your brand by forming alliances with people or companies that want to emulate your achievements.

12. Customer Loyalty Programs: - To keep and reward current customers, put in place customer loyalty programs.

Encouraging recurring business can support long-term expansion.

Through a methodical assessment of these expansion prospects, business owners may develop a thorough plan for growing their side project into a profitable enterprise. Unlocking sustainable growth requires a thorough understanding of market dynamics, innovation, and strategic decision-making.

Building a Team for Your Business

Creating a competent and driven workforce is essential when turning your side project into a company. Take into account the subsequent actions to form and strengthen a productive team:

1. Define Roles and Responsibilities:

- Clearly state each team member's position and responsibilities.

- Verify congruence with both personal and organizational strengths.

2. Identify Core Competencies:

- Determine the fundamental skills required for every position.

- Align knowledge, abilities, and experience with the demands of the company.

3. Hiring and Recruiting:

- To draw in top personnel, carry out a comprehensive hiring procedure.

Evaluate not just abilities but also congruence with the corporate vision and cultural fit.

4. Cultivate a Positive Culture:

- Promote an upbeat and welcoming work environment.

- Promote an atmosphere that values cooperation, creativity, and candid communication.

5. Leadership Development:

- Make an investment in the team's leadership development.

- As the company expands, provide team members the opportunity to assume leadership positions.

6. Effective Communication:

- Provide unambiguous lines of contact.

 - Share expectations, comments, and business updates on a regular basis.

7. Training and Skill Development: - Offer chances for continuous training and skill improvement.

 - Keep the group informed about emerging technology and market trends.

8. Create a Collaborative Environment:

- Encourage team members to work together.

- Promote cooperation, exchange of ideas, and cross-functional coordination.

9. Design Performance Measures:

- Establish KPIs, or key performance indicators, for every role.

- Regularly assess results in relation to these indicators.

CHAPTER 8

Planning for financial freedom

This chapter, "Planning for Financial Freedom," delves into the calculated measures and factors to take into account when working on your side projects and company ventures to become financially independent. Readers will learn how to lay a strong financial foundation by exploring topics such as debt management, long-term financial planning, investing methods, and budgeting. The chapter's mission is to enable people to make wise choices that advance their financial well-being as individuals and as entrepreneurs.

Establishing Financial Independence Goals:

One of the most important parts of preparing for financial independence through your side gig and business is setting strategic, well-defined goals. **Here's an organized method for creating goals:**

1. Clearly Specify Your Goals:

- Clearly state what your financial goals are. Specificity is essential when setting goals for investments, savings, or debt reduction.

2. Brief-Term and Long-Term Objectives:

- Make a distinction between brief and long-term objectives.

Monthly savings targets are an example of a short-term goal; significant investments or retirement planning are examples of long-term goals.

Using the SMART criteria (Specific, Measurable, Achievable, Relevant, Time-bound) to every goal is the third step.

This guarantees that your objectives are precise and attainable.

3. Prioritize Goals:

- Sort your financial objectives according to their significance and urgency.

This facilitates efficient resource allocation and focus.

4. Financial Health Assessment:

- Evaluate your present financial condition.

- Recognize your sources of income, costs, assets, and liabilities to help you develop goals.

5. Emergency Fund:

- Make setting up an emergency fund a top concern.

  - To create a safety net of funds, aim for a fund that can sustain several months' worth of living expenditures.

6. Debt Reduction Targets:

- If appropriate, establish goals for cutting and getting rid of debt.

- Give high-interest loans first priority and make a plan for their gradual payback.

8. Savings Milestones:

- Set aside time to save money.

- This could involve setting aside money for particular expenditures, potential investments, or other financial goals.

9. Investment Goals:

- Specify your financial goals.

- Take into account variables including anticipated returns, investment horizon, and risk tolerance.

10. Business Growth Objectives: - If applicable, include objectives for growing your side hustle or business.

- This could include goals for customer acquisition, revenue targets, or expansion strategies.

Financial Planning Strategies for Side Hustle and Business Success

Making long-term financial plans is crucial to the success of any side project and business. Think about these essential financial planning techniques:

1. **Budgeting**: Make a detailed budget that details your income, spending, and savings objectives.

- Monitor your spending on a regular basis and make adjustments based on real financial results.

2. Emergency Fund: Give creating and keeping an emergency fund top priority.

- Aim for a minimum of three to six months' worth of living expenses to cover unanticipated costs.

3. Debt Management: Create a strategy for overseeing and minimizing debt.

- Give high-interest debts priority, and if appropriate, take debt consolidation techniques into account.

4. Diversify revenue Streams:

Look into and mix different sources of revenue.

- Financial stability is provided by diversification; relying too much on one source of income can be dangerous.

5. Tax Planning: Keep up with tax laws that apply to your company.

   - To reduce tax liabilities, maximize tax deductions and credits.

6. Retirement Planning: - Put a retirement savings strategy into action.

   - Make regular contributions to retirement accounts while utilizing tax-favored options.

7. Insurance Coverage: Determine and obtain sufficient insurance protection.

In order to reduce risks, this comprises health, business, and disability insurance.

8. Investment Portfolio: Create a well-rounded portfolio of investments that is in line with your financial objectives.

- Depending on your time horizon and risk tolerance, think about a combination of stocks, bonds, and other assets

9. Regular Financial checks: Evaluate progress by doing regular financial checks.

- Modify your plans in response to evolving situations, shifting market dynamics, and individual objectives.

10. Savings for Business Growth: - Set aside money expressly for the expansion of your company.

Set aside savings to support business development, whether

they be for product line expansion or marketing campaigns.

11. Negotiate Expenses: Review and bargain for business expenses on a regular basis.

Investigate ways to cut costs without sacrificing effectiveness or quality.

12. Expert Financial Guidance: Speak with accountants or financial experts.

- Seeking professional advice can guarantee adherence to financial best practices and offer insightful information.

Using these money management techniques will help your side gig and business become more stable and profitable. To keep yourself on track toward your objectives and experience long-term financial success, review and modify your financial plan on a regular basis.

Conclusion

To sum up, "Side Hustles and Passive Income" examines the ever-changing world of entrepreneurship and offers guidance to those aiming for success and financial independence. This booklet is a thorough handbook that covers everything from creating, expanding, and maintaining a business to comprehending the intricacies of side gigs and passive income.

The journey that readers take in includes topics such as the significance and definition of side gigs, various sources of money, and methods for evaluating talents and interests. The book walks readers through the complexities of starting a side business, including business planning, legal issues, and web presence.

The booklet explores the possibilities of investing in stocks, real estate, digital goods, and investments as a means of generating passive income. It offers advice on how to manage both full-time employment and side projects while stressing time management techniques and burnout prevention tactics.

Readers receive motivation and useful insights from case studies, success stories, and interviews with people who have perfected the art of side gigs. The booklet finishes with advice on overcoming obstacles and growing a side gig into a long-term, profitable business, along with financial planning techniques. With this newfound understanding, readers will be able to successfully negotiate the challenges of entrepreneurship and realize their goals. The ebook is a dependable travel companion on the road to financial independence and fulfillment as the entrepreneurial journey unfolds.

9 798879 260212